COOL CATS

Persians

by Rebecca Felix

BELLWETHER MEDIA • MINNEAPOLIS, MN

Note to Librarians, Teachers, and Parents:

Blastoff! Readers are carefully developed by literacy experts and combine standards-based content with developmentally appropriate text.

Level 1 provides the most support through repetition of high-frequency words, light text, predictable sentence patterns, and strong visual support.

Level 2 offers early readers a bit more challenge through varied simple sentences, increased text load, and less repetition of high-frequency words.

Level 3 advances early-fluent readers toward fluency through increased text and concept load, less reliance on visuals, longer sentences, and more literary language.

Level 4 builds reading stamina by providing more text per page, increased use of punctuation, greater variation in sentence patterns, and increasingly challenging vocabulary.

Level 5 encourages children to move from "learning to read" to "reading to learn" by providing even more text, varied writing styles, and less familiar topics.

Whichever book is right for your reader, Blastoff! Readers are the perfect books to build confidence and encourage a love of reading that will last a lifetime!

This edition first published in 2016 by Bellwether Media, Inc.

No part of this publication may be reproduced in whole or in part without written permission of the publisher. For information regarding permission, write to Bellwether Media, Inc., Attention: Permissions Department, 5357 Penn Avenue South, Minneapolis, MN 55419.

Library of Congress Cataloging-in-Publication Data

Felix, Rebecca, 1984- author.
 Persians / by Rebecca Felix.
     pages cm. – (Blastoff! Readers. Cool Cats)
   Summary: "Relevant images match informative text in this introduction to Persian cats. Intended for students in kindergarten through third grade"– Provided by publisher.
 Audience: Ages 5-8
 Audience: K to grade 3
 Includes bibliographical references and index.
 ISBN 978-1-62617-233-3 (hardcover: alk. paper)
 1. Persian cat–Juvenile literature. I. Title.
 SF449.P4F45 2016
 636.8'32–dc23

                        2015004747

Table of Contents

What Are Persians?

Persians are long-haired cats.

Their soft fur is the longest of any cat **breed**.

A Persian has a short, flat **muzzle**.

muzzle

It sometimes looks squished in!

Persians come from **ancient** Persia. Today, this country is called Iran.

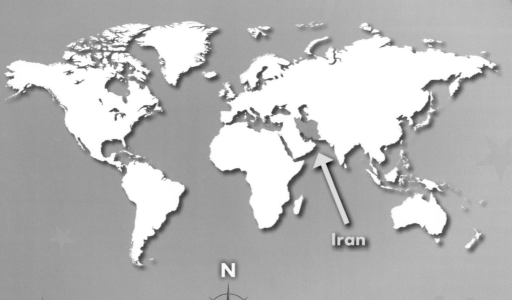

Iran

N
W E
S

These cats were brought to
Europe in the 1600s. European
royalty kept them as pets.

The breed came to the
United States in the 1800s.

They are now one of the most popular cat breeds in the world!

Fluffy and Round

Silky Persian **coats** can be **solid** colors, such as white or black. Smoke coats have a hidden white **undercoat**.

Persian Coats

solid

smoke

bi-color

tabby

Persians can also be **bi-color** or **tabby**.

These cats have round eyes and faces. Their eyes are often orange. Some have blue or green eyes.

Persian ears are rounded
and short.

A Persian's body is medium to large in size. It sits atop short legs. The cat's tail is short, too. But it is covered in long, fluffy hair!

Persian Profile

— short, round ears

— flat face and nose

— long, silky hair

Weight: 7 to 14 pounds (3 to 6 kilograms)

Life Span: 10 to 15 years

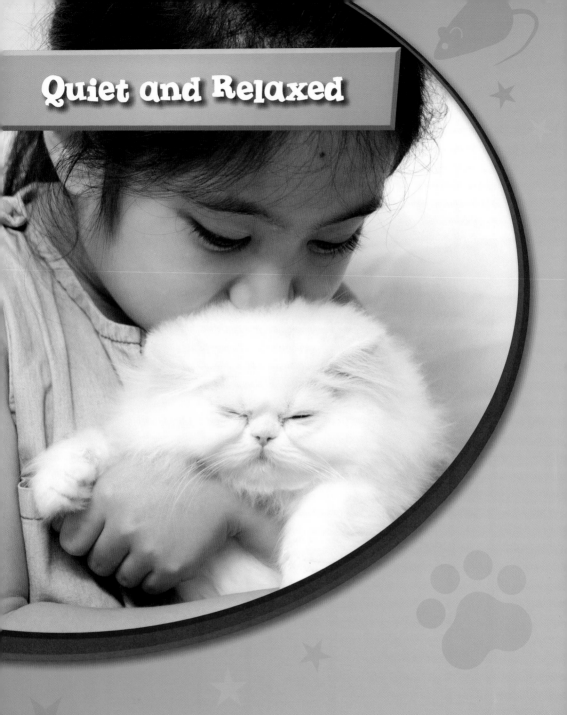

Quiet and Relaxed

Persians are relaxed and sweet.
They like **affection**.

Owners need to give Persians a lot of attention and care. Their coats must be brushed daily.

Persians are known as
the quietest cat breed.

These calm cats do not usually jump or climb. They will sleep and **lounge** on furniture all day!

Glossary

affection—love and care

ancient—from long ago

bi-color—a pattern that has two fur colors, one being white

breed—a type of cat

coats—the hair or fur covering some animals

lounge—to sit or rest in a lazy manner

muzzle—the nose and mouth of an animal

royalty—kings and queens

silky—soft, smooth, and shiny

solid—one color

tabby—a pattern that has stripes, patches, or swirls of colors

undercoat—a layer of short fur underneath an outer layer of longer fur

To Learn More

AT THE LIBRARY

Markovics, Joyce L. *Persians: Long-Haired Friends.* New York, N.Y.: Bearport, 2011.

Micco, Trudy. *Discover Persian Cats.* Berkeley Heights, N.J.: Enslow Publishers, 2012.

Owen, Ruth. *Persians.* New York, N.Y.: PowerKids Press, 2014.

ON THE WEB

Learning more about Persians is as easy as 1, 2, 3.

1. Go to www.factsurfer.com.

2. Enter "Persians" into the search box.

3. Click the "Surf" button and you will see a list of related web sites.

With factsurfer.com, finding more information is just a click away.

Index